ON EAGLES' WINGS

How to let Jesus bear your burdens

formerly published as
"Weight" on the Lord

RANDY MAXWELL

Pacific Press® Publishing Association
Nampa, Idaho
Oshawa, Ontario, Canada

Lovingly dedicated to my wife Suzette, who—with me—continues daily to discover the faithfulness of a God who never sleeps, the possibility of the "impossible," and the thrill of "high flight" in Jesus. (Honey, "you're the wind beneath my wings.")

And to Mom and Dad who always believed in me, taught me to "follow through," and allowed me the freedom to "dream on!"

And also to my God, who knows me through and through—and loves me anyway!

Edited by Ken McFarland
Designed by Dennis Ferree
Cover photo by John W. Warden/Superstock
Typeset in 10/12 Century Schoolbook

Copyright © 1986 by
Pacific Press® Publishing Association
Printed in the United States of America
All Rights Reserved

Library of Congress Cataloging in Publication Date

Maxwell, Randy.
   "Weight" on the Lord and Soar On Eagles' Wings

  1. Trust in God—Christianity. I. Title
BV4637.M35   1986   248.4   85-17036
ISBN 0-8163-1345-8

Contents

"Weight," I Say, on the Lord!	5
The One Minute Christian	10
Chicken's Feet in Strait Places	17
"How Great Thou Art!—Sometimes"	25
Take a Praise Break	32
"Shhh—"	37
In Paths of Righteousness	47
On Eagle's Wings	56

"Weight," I Say, on the Lord!

"Just wait on the Lord, brother," or "Look to Jesus" are common expressions in and around the body of Christ—and if you have been a Christian for any substantial length of time, you, like me, have heard them a "million" times. They have to rank at least second or third among the Top Ten favorite Christian clichés.

Want proof? The next time you're facing a trial or find yourself in some kind of trouble, see how much time elapses before someone offers these words of "comfort" to you. But don't go to sleep while you wait, because they're coming at you—count on it. And you know what? When *someone else*—a friend, relative, co-worker, or fellow believer—gets in trouble, they'll hear them too—from *you*.

Now don't get me wrong. I'm in no way poking fun at what I believe to be one of the greatest promises of Scripture. See Isaiah 40:31. It's just that I've found that we Christians, always anxious to give "the answer," glibly spout off this verse, applying it to another's trial with all the finesse of a rapid-fire machine gun, without really comprehending what it is we're saying or what the Bible is really saying. I know I didn't—not really. I discovered that it's

6 "WEIGHT" ON THE LORD

EASY to wait on the Lord. That's right, easy—until—*until I had to wait on Him!*

When the bills are paid and you have just received that new promotion, your car is running like a Swiss watch, physically you've never felt better, and generally life is handing you a bouquet of roses, waiting on God is a snap! But just let the car break down or the funds get a little tight or let the bill collectors start inviting themselves over for dinner, and suddenly you're bleeding from the thorns on that bouquet of roses life just handed you. There you stand, blood flowing from your fingertips, and some well-meaning "saint" is grinning in your face telling you to "Hang in there. We'll understand it better by and by. Just *WAIT.*"

Allow me to pause right here and say that most of us Christians don't realize that good timing is just as important as good counsel, and all too often we plunge the scalpel into the wound before the patient is properly anesthetized! Timing is crucial, and at that moment, those well-meant words—because of how they've been misused and misunderstood—are probably the last ones you want to hear.

It reminds me of taking a hot shower. If you're like me, you love the way a hot shower relaxes and warms you all over. The feel of the warm stream on your skin is delicious. It loosens you up, and for the moment, you feel calm, tranquil, mellow. You may even start singing the praises of God. Warm water gives a different perspective on life. Everything is going fine until somebody else in the apartment complex, at that particular moment, also decides to enjoy a hot shower. The water pressure suddenly decreases, and you know what's coming next, don't you? The songs of praise are interrupted by a shriek of anger, and if it weren't for the grace of God operating in your life, words you wouldn't admit are in your vocabulary would spew out of your mouth. Yikes! The water is ice-cold! "Hey, cut it out! That's not fair!" you yell. (If you don't, I sure do!) And imagine your reaction if that "other" person were to yell back, "Wait!" At that moment, with ice-cold water shocking your body, I doubt if, "OK, God bless you—and have a nice day," would be your reply. Yet when we're hurting the most, we're told to "wait."

But just what is *waiting* on the Lord? How does it work? Is there really more to it than just "grinning and bearing it?" Can we finally take it from the Top Ten cliché list and find some practical application for it to our marriages, our finances, our automobiles—our very lives?

It is because I believe there is a positive answer to these questions that I have entitled this book *"Weight," on the Lord,* spelled W-E-I-G-H-T. I have done so because I truly believe that when the Lord tells us to "wait," He has more in mind for His children than just sitting in a corner with our Bibles, wringing our hands. Or walking around with a plastic smile on our faces, lying to everyone who asks, "How are you today?" by answering, "Fine"—while inside we resemble a piece of chewed meat—torn up with fear, anxiety, and hurt.

No, I believe the Lord wants us to W-E-I-G-H-T on Him—to place the full weight of our burden, whatever it is, totally on Him and thereby receive a fresh supply of strength to continue on. Is this not what the apostle Peter means with these words?

Cast all your anxiety on him because he cares for you. 1 Peter 5:7, NIV.

Jesus has been very up front and honest with His followers regarding trials and suffering. He assures us that as long as we are still in this world we will have tribulation. Nevertheless, He adds the consolation that because of His triumph over sin, Satan, and the grave, we can be of good cheer. See John 16:33. We can have hope and actually learn the secret of transforming our desert experiences into watered gardens of faith and trust in a God who has promised never to leave or forsake us.

Jesus has spread out a banquet table of blessings for His children, and far too many of us have spent the majority of our Christian lives wasting away on the crumbs—and all because we won't "taste and see that the Lord is good." Psalm 34:8. We don't put God's Word to the test and practically apply its counsel to our everyday lives. As a result, we may be twenty or thirty years old in our Christian walk with a kindergarten faith that remains stunted and immature from lack of use.

It has been said that when we get to heaven, we'll be surprised to find a room full of unopened, gift-wrapped boxes with our names on them and cards attached that read:

NEVER DELIVERED TO EARTH, BECAUSE NEVER REQUESTED FROM EARTH.

These boxes contain all the promises and spiritual weapons of God's Word that could have been ours in times of need but were never claimed, never applied.

Jesus is anxiously waiting for His children to experience more that just a theoretical, intellectual relationship with Him, and all heaven waits to bestow on us all the glorious fullness of the living Christ.

"WEIGHT," I SAY, ON THE LORD! 9

We need but to ask, and the experience will be ours.

I believe it was never the Lord's intent for us to grovel through this life, eking out a meager existence, just "hanging in there" until He would come and take us home to heaven. Sorry, that's not the picture my Bible paints for me.

> *The Lord shall make thee the head, and not the tail; and thou shalt be above only, and thou shalt not be beneath.* Deuteronomy 28:13.

Jesus wants us to be "more than conquerors" (see Romans 8:37), and we *can* get "above" our trials and soar above our difficulties. But before we can "mount up with wings as eagles," we must drop our "turkey" mentality and "WEIGHT" on Him.

This book doesn't pretend to have all the answers. Times of perplexity and doubt will still come (I know—I've had them in the publication of this book)! Nor does this book seek to eliminate all trouble. Rather, it attempts to provide some positive, practical, biblical methods of coping with the many trials we face from day to day. I offer the next few pages of ink and paper as a sacrifice to God and a gift to you with a prayer that the simple words and thoughts shared herein will help you strengthen your grip on the hand of God—in the valley as well as on the mountaintop—and learn how, *by faith*, to "run, and not be weary; . . . walk, and not faint."

"WEIGHT," I say, on the Lord!

The One Minute Christian

In July of '83 I was blessed of God with a promotion on my job. I had been an intermediate typist clerk in the physical therapy department of Rancho Los Amigos Hospital, Downey, California, for two years—and after passing a county-wide exam, I was promoted to supervisor.

Wanting to become a superb manager, I began attending seminars and reading books on how to become a good supervisor. One of the books I enjoyed most was a small book entitled *The One Minute Manager*. Maybe you've read it. In an allegory format, the book sets forth three simple management skills that promise to increase productivity, profits, job satisfaction, and personal prosperity while taking only one minute each to implement. They are one minute goal settings, one minute praisings, and one minute reprimands.

The authors guarantee success if these skills are implemented and further declare that these same principles can be helpful in settings other than business. Now this is not a commercial for *The One Minute Manager*, but honestly, after reading the book, I'd have to agree that the principles can work in most situations. But I don't think the authors ever

THE ONE MINUTE CHRISTIAN 11

dreamed their concepts would catch on so fast and influence the behavior patterns of so many. Why, not only are one minute managers flourishing throughout the business world, but look around the church today and you'll see a bumper crop of one minute *Christians* springing up all over the place! And don't look too many pews down—you may be one of them. I was! (Did I say "was"?)

What is a one minute Christian? Allow me to illustrate. Ever read God's "Faith Hall of Fame" in Hebrews 11? What an inspiration! God's champions—their deeds of faith and experience forever captured on the film of ink and paper for us to learn from and imitate. As we mentally walk down these sacred halls, admiring the word portraits describing the exploits of these spiritual giants, we pause at our favorites and linger as if to drink in those traits of character we admire most.

Three of my favorites are Abraham, Joseph, and Moses. Abraham enjoyed such a rich relationship with the Creator that God gave him the highest honor by calling him "My friend." See Isaiah 41:8. Joseph, by remaining firm as rock to principle, refusing to dishonor God in any way, was exalted to the second highest position in the royal courts of Egypt. And Moses, unlike anyone before or since, enjoyed such an intimate, personal relationship with Jehovah that to him was granted the incredible privilege of talking to God, "face to face, as a man speaketh unto his friend." Exodus 33:11.

"O Lord," I've often prayed, "I want to be like that! Please give me faith like Moses, the steadfastness and virtue of Joseph, and the experience of Abraham." Sound familiar? Sure it does. We've all prayed prayers like that—and do you know HOW we wanted those prayers to be answered? We wished that God would whip out some kind of huge, celestial funnel, stick one end in our ears, and pour the ingredients of spiritual greatness down the other end. Now, we don't consciously think about it happening that way, but our attitudes in the face of a crisis, or when we have to wait for something we really want, reveal that subconsciously this is exactly the way we want it.

Want proof? Remember the last time you prayed for patience, and the car wouldn't start that morning, you were late for church, and *you* were on the program? Remember? How did you react? Were the words, "be anxious for nothing" on your lips? Well I'll be honest, I had some words for the Lord all right, but not those. "Lord, You know I'm late for church, and I know that for You, fixing a VW is no big deal—so why don't You fix it! Now! After all, I'm just trying to do *YOUR* work in *YOUR* house for *YOUR* people!"

After some yelling, some pounding, more conversation with the Lord, and repeated threats of sending my car on a vacation over the side of Point Fermen, the car would start, and my wife would gently remind me that I really had no right getting angry. "After all," she would smirk, "you prayed for patience." Well, Honey, if this is the way I'm going to get it—KEEP IT! Ooops. Without even knowing it, I had met my first one minute Christian—me!

You see, we live in a society where everybody wants everything quick and in a hurry. Instant coffee, instant breakfast, fast foods, quickie divorces, trial marriages, rush-hour traffic, one-day paint centers, three-minute eggs, twenty-minute workouts, and one minute managers. Now all of this speed is not *all* bad. But when the "instant" attitude creeps into the church, you've got problems.

Many Christians today want their spiritual food "to go." Clocks are in prominent places in the sanctuary, and bells and chimes are set to go off when "time's up." And even if the pastor is in mid-sentence, he'd better sit down when the gong sounds, or he'll be left preaching to pews! Because there is such a push for time, all the pastor can really get out are "sermonettes," which, as my former pastor jokingly said, produce only "Christianettes."

Five minutes a day in the Word (if that much), a few scattered minutes in prayer (if we remember to), ninety minutes max at church once a week, and we want to have great experiences with God. We want, to coin a phrase, to "have it our way"—and our way is quick and easy.

Surprise! That's not how God's champions of faith did it. How did they achieve their great faith, their great relationship with Jehovah? Brace yourselves, fellow one minuters—they had to WAIT. That's right. These faith-hall-of-famers were not only "heavyweights" in the kingdom of God—they were "heavy*waits*" as well.

Take Moses, for starters. His training for the tremendous job of leading the children of Israel from Egypt to Canaan took place in the desert of Midian, tending sheep, of all things. And he tended sheep for forty years! (And you think your job is boring!) Then after he led his people to the very gates of the Promised Land, they refused to believe the land was theirs, so God sent them and Moses back into the desert for forty *more* years. Think of seeing nothing but sand, rocks, cactus, and ornery people day in and day out for forty years! (The sheep were a piece of cake compared to this!) Think Moses ever experienced boredom or burnout?

Abraham had to wait until he was a hundred years old before he received the son God had promised him years before. And Joseph had to languish in the Egyptian dungeon for two years before he was elevated to his high position before Pharaoh. Why? Why did they have to go through such experiences? Because in order to develop faith, faith must be exercised. And waiting is the spiritual exercise program prescribed to develop muscles of faith. There are no shortcuts to spiritual maturity. The Bible describes it as a process.

First the blade, then the ear, after that the full corn in the ear. Mark 4:28.

This experience, however, we'd prefer to skip. Forget all those tedious years of classwork—*just hand over the diploma!*

I saw a TV commercial recently that illustrates this attitude perfectly. The product being advertised was a weight-loss pill called Dream-Away. What supposedly makes this product unique is its claim to help you lose weight as you sleep. That's right! You send the company $19.95, and they'll send you Dream-Away so you can start shedding pounds in your sleep "without tiresome exercise." I laugh every time I see that commercial because it mirrors so beautifully our free-lunch, give-it-to-me-easy, get-rich-thin-beautiful-*anything*-quick attitude. We want the ends without the means—the crown but not the cross.

This one minute attitude is dangerous to Christians because it robs us of an essential character trait we must have if we're to survive the coming crisis. Listen to what one Christian writer has to say about this.

> *The "time of trouble, such as never was," is soon to open upon us; and we shall need an experience which we do not now possess and which many are too indolent [lazy] to obtain.*—Ellen G. White, *The Great Controversy*, p. 622.

And again on page 621:

> *The season of distress and anguish before us will require a faith that can endure weariness, delay, and hunger—a faith that will not faint though severely tried.*

We need endurance—the ability to wait on God "continually" (see Hosea 12:6), depending solely on His sovereign word and power to help us in every trial and every situation. This is what the writer to the Hebrews meant when he said:

> *You need to persevere so that when you have done the will of God, you will receive what he has promised. For in a very little while, "he who is coming will come and will not delay. But my righteous one will live by faith. And if he shrinks back, I will not be pleased with him."* Hebrews 10:36-38, NIV.

You can't jump in water without getting wet, and you can't learn to endure without enduring. Sorry, there are no shortcuts.

Discouraged? Don't be. The waiting times that God must bring into our lives give us the opportunity to "WEIGHT" on Him and deepen our relationship with Him. Jesus says:

> *Abide in me, and I in you. As the branch cannot bear fruit of itself, except it abide in the vine; no more can ye, except ye abide in me. . . . Without me ye can do nothing.* John 15:4, 5.

"Dwell with Me," Jesus says. "Spend some time in My presence—in My Word—and get to know Me better. I want you to know Me, not just in your head, but in your heart. Taste and see that I am good, that I am faithful, that I am your Provider, your Shepherd, your Rock, your Fortress, your Refuge and Place of quiet rest. *Know* me! Then you will bear fruit and become all I created you to be—My friend—My child!"

What a privilege! To intimately know and experience the Almighty, one-on-one. Is this the kind of relationship you want with God? To know—*really* know and be known of Him? Then pull up a chair and welcome to "WAITING 101"—class is in session!

No, we can't "dream away" our sinful natures—and no, we can't produce the fruit of righteousness in "one minute" or as we sleep. But take heart. Sanctification may be the work of a lifetime, but it takes less than sixty seconds to ask Jesus to forgive our impatience, change our attitudes, and abide in us so that we too can become God's champions, joining those heroes who have gone before us in proclaiming to the world that God lives, God loves, and God reigns. Do it right now. He's waiting.

Chicken's Feet in Strait Places

Hannah Hurnard has written a classic in Christian literature that—if you haven't read already—you must read as soon as possible. (After you've finished this one, of course!) The book is entitled *Hind's Feet on High Places* (Tyndale House Publishers, Inc., 1979). In allegorical style, Hannah relates the story of a young crippled girl named Much Afraid.

Much Afraid belongs to a clan of frightened relatives known as the Fearlings, who reside in the town of Much Trembling in the Valley of Humiliation. (Neat-sounding places, yes?) This Valley of Humiliation is bordered by towering, snow-capped mountains, the peaks of which comprise the Kingdom of Love, residence of the Chief Shepherd, otherwise known as Christ. The Shepherd meets twice daily with Much Afraid and invites her to come with Him to the "high places," there to find true love and to be given "hind's feet" in place of her crippled ones.

The hind is a female red deer and is known for her surefootedness and amazing agility in scaling the steepest mountain faces and treacherous cliffs. With an ease that defies comprehension, the hind leaps effortlessly from ledge to ledge, accurately tracking the hoofprints of her male companion, who leads the way. The Chief Shepherd also possessed this amazing ability, and Much Afraid longed to have these swift, supple feet that would allow her to go skipping and bounding across the lofty peaks all the way to the high places, far beyond the reach of her troublesome relatives.

Without telling you the whole story, I'll summarize the point which is simply this: In her quest for the "high places," Much Afraid encounters many "strait" places—setbacks, "tight spots," "potholes," if you will—in the straight and narrow pathway. At these places of trial along the way, she learns to surrender, trust the Shepherd, and finally develop hind's feet—as well as the ability to overcome her fears. It is a moving story of what faith in and waiting on God is all about.

However, Much Afraid doesn't learn these lessons all at once—oh, no! She's Much Afraid, remember? Her early responses to the strait places she finds herself in could be better described as panic, terror, and dread. But the Chief Shepherd knows what He is doing. You see, before Much Afraid can have hind's feet on high places, she has to overcome her *chicken's feet in the strait places!* And so do we! If we want to walk with Christ in the heavenlies, we must learn to walk with Him in the valleys.

Ask yourself, "How do *I* respond to the strait places in my life?" What happens to my peace of mind, my joy, my "blessed assurance," when I'm in a bind—when pesky problems seem to be crowding in on me? I think if we're honest, we'll agree that our response is very much like that of Saul's army at Gilgal.

The story unfolds in 1 Samuel 13. The Israeli army, under the command of Saul, had just returned from a mighty victory over their enemies, the Ammonites. Saul assembled the people at Gilgal, where he was anointed king. Brimming with confidence, he disbanded the army, reserving only 2,000 men under his command at Michmash and 1,000 under the command of his son, Jonathan, at Gibeah.

In the second year of Saul's reign, an attempt was made to subdue another of Israel's enemies, the Philistines. Son Jonathan led his troops in a sneak attack against a garrison of Philistine troops at Geba. The Philistine people heard of the attack, and they weren't too happy about it. Just look at how they planned to get even:

The Philistines gathered themselves together to fight with Israel, thirty thousand chariots, and six thousand horsemen, and people as the sand which is on the sea shore in multitude. Verse 5.

Talk about retaliation! They weren't playing! But how did the brave children of Israel respond? After all, they had whipped the Ammonites and witnessed many other evidences of God's awesome might. Just how did God's chosen people react?

When the men of Israel saw that they were in a strait, (for the people were distressed,) then the people [Prayed, right? Wrong.] *did hide themselves in caves, and in thickets, and in rocks, and in high places, and in pits.* Verse 6.

They were indeed in a strait place, and if you had been there, you might have choked on the cloud of feathers they left in their wake as Israelites scattered in every possible direction, running for their very lives! They looked eyeball to eyeball with that overwhelming army, and the only battle cry heard that day was "RUN!" There they were, the royal priesthood, the holy nation, the children of God, quaking in their boots and ducking for cover behind anything that wouldn't move—bushes, caves, rocks, even empty tombs! The Bible paints an even more vivid picture for us in verse 7 when it describes the people as "trembling."

What happened? Hadn't God wrought wonderfully for them in the past? Hadn't Israel overcome tremendous odds under the power of Jehovah before? Certainly. Then why the "chicken's feet" instead of "hind's feet"? Don't ask it of the children of Israel unless you also plan to ask it of yourself. What happened to them is what happens to us more often than we'd like to admit when we find ourselves in a "strait." We take our eyes off God—the first mistake—and place them squarely on the problem—the second mistake.

It has always amazed me how soon the Israelites forgot how God miraculously made a freeway through the Red Sea for them and how, in no time at all, they doubted His ability to take care of their most basic needs. After a big victory dance on the other side of the Red Sea, the Bible says:

Moses brought Israel from the Red sea . . . ; and they went three days in the wilderness, and found no water. Exodus 15:22.

No problem, right? Surely this God who can part oceans and whom I can see with my very own eyes leading the way, disguised in a cloud by day and a pillar of fire by night, can easily provide a little

Perrier for me to drink. No biggie.

And when they came to Marah, they could not drink of the waters..., for they were bitter. Verse 23.

Uh, oh. Here's all the water they can drink, but it's not Perrier.

And the people murmured against Moses, saying, What shall we drink? Verse 24.

"Where's the Perrier, Lord? I knew You couldn't pull this off. I was better off in Egypt! At least there you can get some decent water when you're thirsty. I bet I look real intelligent out here in the desert with no canteen! How am I supposed to survive? Can't You see that this is the desert? I'm thirsty!"

Forgotten was the Red Sea celebration just seventy-two hours earlier. Forgotten were the plagues of Egypt that had broken Pharaoh's hard heart and caused him to let them go. Only one thing was on their minds—*water*, and they couldn't care less what God had done yesterday.

Don't smile too much now. When was the last time you were facing an overwhelming situation and panicked? I remember just a few months ago, I was involved in a "fender bender" that, unfortunately, was my fault. My 1971 VW had somehow decided to make acquaintance with the front fender of a late-model Cadillac (of all cars!), and I was faced with a $600 repair bill. I could have let my insurance company take care of it—if I had been insured. What made matters worse was that my car was already in desperate need of repair. I was behind on some other bills, and my wife and I were at that time trying to move into a larger apartment.

I was in a "strait" (A MESS in today's vernacular). But not to worry. I had FAITH! God had proven Himself again and again in our marriage, and I was going to WAIT on His provision and trust His leading. After all, He allowed the accident to happen, right? So I knew He was in control, and all I had to do was believe He'd send the money.

Days turned into weeks, and after much prayer—still no $600. The bills were still behind, and I was getting nervous. (The Philistines were gathering their army!) I thought I would *help* get things going, so I applied for a loan that would more than cover my immediate needs and ease our other bill pressures considerably. I felt good. This had to be *God's* solution to our problem. There just wasn't *any other way* that *I* could see.

The loan didn't come through. I sounded the battle cry—"RUN!" "God, where are You? Can't You see the trouble I'm in? Now what am I going to do? Don't You care? Don't You understand?" Cluck. Cluck.

Forgotten were the Lord's blessings of the past. Forgotten were the numerous times of deliverance before. I saw the overwhelming "armies" of financial obligations and "trembled."

Just how are we, as Christians, as sons and daughters of the King, to respond to the strait places in life? Well, David faced many strait places in his life. How did he deal with them? In 2 Samuel 24, we're told the story of David's sin in numbering the people of Israel. The Lord was angry with David, and through a prophet named Gad, God gave David a choice between three punishments. Choice one: seven years of famine. Choice two: running from enemies for three months. Choice three: three days of pestilence in the land. David was, to put it mildly, "between a rock and a hard place!" What did he do? I love David's response! It is the essence of what this book is all about.

David said unto God, I am in a great strait:—

And here's the part I love—

Let us fall now into the hand of the Lord; for his mercies are great. Verse 14.

Did you see that? David's response to his strait place was to "fall" into the hand of the Lord. He W-E-I-G-H-T-E-D on the Lord!

Friend, the "high places" of joy and peace are only a "strait" place away! The times we spend in the valley—how we spend them—will determine the time we spend on the mountaintop, and the transformation begins as soon as we stop running and start falling "into the hand of the Lord." We do this by taking our needs to God in prayer and by taking our eyes off the problem and putting them on the Word.

The kind of prayers we need to be praying are those based on the promises in God's Word. Pray according to the appropriate promise for your particular situation, and then, by all means, *believe* what it says and start rejoicing in the victory. Don't waste time and energy focusing on the problem. You already know what the problem is and so does God. So don't be like Chicken Little, crying, "the sky is falling, the sky is falling!" Concentrate on the Word. Talk victory and talk faith, and your faith will grow and your strength will be renewed.

Then keep moving forward. When the children of Israel were trapped between the Egyptian army and the Red Sea, God's order was that the people "go forward." While we wait on the Lord for deliverance, we're not to sit around wringing our hands. Stay active. Get involved in someone else's life. Participate in ministries that nurture and reach out to others. Continue knocking on doors with expectancy, and the promised answer will come.

Much Afraid eventually reached the high places and received hind's feet in place of her crippled ones. She reached the high places because she learned to fall "into the hand of the Lord"—to WEIGHT on Him in the strait places. How about it? Ready to trade in the chicken's feet and start walking in victory? One thing is for sure, we'll not be disappointed. God promises that—

They shall not be ashamed that wait for me. Isaiah 49:23.

By the way, I can testify to the truth of this promise. Through circumstances I never would have dreamed of, God—in the span of three weeks—more than met our need. He gave us the $600 and then some, and we're still praising His name!

Put God to the test. *Claim* the promises for a change, instead of just reading them. Despite what you think, they *are* for *you*. Start falling into the hands of the Lord, and you'll be well on your way to developing the feet of the hind in the high places.

See you at the top!

"How Great Thou Art!— Sometimes"

O Lord my God! When I in awesome wonder,
  Consider all the worlds Thy hands have made,
I see the stars, I hear the rolling thunder,
  Thy Pow'r throughout the universe displayed.

When through the woods and forest glades I wander,
  And hear the birds sing sweetly in the trees;
When I look down from lofty mountain grandeur,
  And hear the brook, and feel the gentle breeze—

Then sings my soul, My Savior God, to Thee;
  "How great Thou art, How great Thou art."

These beautiful words depicting the awesome majesty of our Lord never cease to inspire reverent wonder and amazement within the heart of all true believers. Stuart K. Hine seemed to have been lifted to the heavens and given a live interview with the Creator, capturing on paper the glory and magnificent power of the One who "spake, and it was done," who "commanded, and it stood fast." Psalm 33:9. I especially identify with the part about the stars.

Ever since I can remember, I've had a fascination

with astronomy. In my earlier years I was constantly asking my dad to take me to the public library, where I would check out as many books as they would allow about space travel, the universe, star systems, and rockets. I dreamed of growing up one day to become an astronaut—and, if asked, I could have told you the exact distance from the moon to the earth, how many days the trip there and back would take, the names of each major part of the lunar exploration module, command module, and three-stage *Saturn V* booster rocket; what kind of fuel it burned; how much it weighed; the amount of thrust produced by its mammoth engines; and the escape velocity needed to leave our atmosphere. I felt as if I knew astronauts Collins, Aldrin, and Armstrong (the first men on the moon—in case you didn't remember) personally. I would turn my little handheld telescope toward the moon and long to be up there with them.

I had a close friend who shared my passion for the stars, and together we would build and launch homemade rockets made from the cardboard tubes found in the center of toilet-paper rolls. We even went so far as to design "serious" blueprints for a real rocket we would build using an old World War II bombshell we had acquired.

I still remember the night I really "saw" the stars for the very first time. Being born and raised in Los Angeles, I hadn't really seen stars—outside of the handful normally visible in southern California skies. The brightness of the city lights, coupled with southland smog, makes star gazing difficult at best. However, in the summer of 1970, my parents sent me away to camp at Camp Cedar Falls, which is situated at about the 6,000-foot level in the San

"HOW GREAT THOU ART!—SOMETIMES"

Bernardino mountains. I was eleven years old and away from home for the first time.

I'll never forget that first night. Supper was over, and most of the campers were making their way to the cabins. About the time I was leaving the cafeteria, a friend of mine yelled out to me, "Hey, Randy, come over to the ballfield. I want to show you something!" I don't mind telling you that I didn't particularly want to go over to the ballfield right then. For one thing, there were no lights on the field—for another, it was dark! I mean *really* dark! (Remember, I was just a naive, sheltered city kid—what did I know about real darkness?) However, being called a "chicken" was far more terrifying than whatever could have been lurking in the dark, so I walked slowly to the spot where my friend was standing, anticipating the practical joke that was sure to come.

"Look up," he said.

I can't remember just what I said when I looked into the San Bernardino night sky, but I'm sure I must have gasped. There, before my eyes, were STARS! Not just a handful, either. Thousands and thousands of stars seemed literally to be popping out all over the place. There were so many it was almost frightening. The scene took my breath away.

I stood there for what seemed like hours, watching all the things I had only read about in books. There was the Milky Way galaxy. Over there was Orion's belt, the Big and Little dippers. I even saw shooting stars! It was glorious. As I stared disbelievingly, trying to grasp the enormity of the heavens, the thought that kept running through my mind was, "God, how great Thou art!" I truly felt like kneeling and worshiping the God who was so wonderful, so magnificent, so awesomely powerful as to have spoken all this into existence.

As Christians, we've all shared similar experiences when looking at the heavens or admiring the detail of a sea shell at the beach or standing next to a giant redwood or beholding the majesty of Yosemite's granite mountains. At those times, God seems to be so big, so wonderful. But what happens when the mountains of Yosemite are out of sight? When the stars of Cedar Falls are swallowed by the neon jungle of the Los Angeles skyline, and the crash of incoming waves is miles away? During times such as these, our "problems" have a funny way of appearing so big, while making our "Great and Powerful" God appear so small.

Amazing, isn't it? How is it that we can be so convinced of God's greatness at some times and so doubtful of His ability to handle the simplest of our problems at other times? Now we would never admit to such thoughts in a crowd of Christians, but what we *do*—our actions and reactions in the midst of trial—makes a statement to the world of how we *really* feel about our heavenly Father. And more times than not, that statement is, "How great Thou art!—sometimes!"

It's as if God is only good for the spectacular and miraculous but inept and ill-equipped when it comes to handling the nitty-gritty of our lives. Oh yes, God can speak worlds into being and can keep the planets in their proper orbits. He can paint the peacock and set boundaries on the sea. He's the Master of earth and sea and sky, *but—can He handle my bank account?*

As Christians, if we are ever going to start experiencing the abundant life that Jesus promised us—a life of victory, fulfillment, indescribable joy, and peace that passes understanding, we're going to have to start believing that God is real and *can* make a difference in our lives as easily and effortlessly as He can create a universe.

It's as my mother always says, "Jesus must be Lord of all, or He's not Lord *at all!*"

We must stop singing the words to our hymns while not listening to what is being said.

'Tis so sweet to trust in Jesus,
*   Just to take Him at His word;*
Just to rest upon His promise,
*   Just to know "thus saith the Lord."*

Is this true in your life—or is it just a bunch of words set to music and used as "filler" in church services?

The Lord's our Rock, in Him we hide,
*   A shelter in the time of storm.*

True or false?

What a friend we have in Jesus,
*   All our sins and griefs to bear;*
What a privilege to carry
*   Everything to God in prayer!*

Is Jesus our friend? Do we carry *everything*—the job, the car, the bills, the kids, the boredom, the depression, the worry, the problem, whatever it is—to Him in prayer, expecting real, honest-to-goodness help?

And what of God's Word?

My God shall supply all your need according to his riches in glory by Christ Jesus. Philippians 4:19.

Fairytales?

I can do all things through Christ which strengtheneth me. Philippians 4:13.

Does it really mean ALL things?

If thou shalt confess with thy mouth the Lord Jesus, and shalt believe in thine heart that God hath raised him from the dead, thou shalt be saved. Romans 10:9.

Not really—not me, anyway.

They that wait upon the Lord shall renew their strength; they shall mount up with wings as eagles; they shall run, and not be weary; and they shall walk, and not faint. Isaiah 40:31.

Just pretty words good only for sermon material and devotional books? I hope that the point of these last couple of chapters is coming through loud and clear. God's Word is more than just a conversation piece, and it's to be put into practice in more situations than just Bible quizzes and memory-verse contests. The Word is real. The Word is life, and unless we start putting it into practice in our everyday lives and situations, we will never learn how to wait on the Lord with any degree of success. And unless we do, we may spend the rest of our Christian lives on

"HOW GREAT THOU ART!—SOMETIMES" 31

this earth defeated, frustrated, and joyless. You don't put your weight on anything that won't support you, and our reluctance to take God at His Word, coupled with a great eagerness to "handle it" ourselves, reveals that deep down, we don't really believe God's promises will hold up.

Don't put off happiness for "that day" when the trump will sound and the Lord shall descend. Jesus wants us to experience heaven now, and, believe it or not, heaven begins as soon as we begin "weighting" on Him—when we begin to believe that God is not just the God of the universe but also the Lord of our lives. No detail in our lives is so small that it escapes His notice. All of our "ins and outs," our "ups and downs" He knows and cares about. So "lean" on Him. He'll hold you up—really He will.

Jesus loves us all so much. Let's allow Him access to our tiny world—our relationships, our occupations, our likes and dislikes, our pleasures, and our pains. If He can order the planets, surely He can order our lives. Let's give Him the chance, at least.

What a God we serve! He creates us from the dust, allows us the prerogative to doubt His power, and yet loves, protects, forgives, and provides for us anyway! Truly how great Thou art!—always and forever!

Take a Praise Break

In chapter 3 we shared a couple of ways we may learn to shift our focus from problem to Problem Solver. I purposely left something out so that more space could be given to it in this chapter.

Before going any further, however, I think now is a good time to make sure I'm not being misunderstood. Sometimes, when people read books like this—books dealing with subjects of faith, trusting God's will, endurance, and victory over fear, anxiety, and stress, the feeling they often come away with when they're finished is *not* peace and tranquility. On the contrary. Sometimes they actually come away feeling guilty and depressed! (Are you nodding?)

This happens because some of these books almost seem to say that if you—as a Christian—ever experience the slightest twinge of anxiety or discouragement, you've all but denied Christ and sinned. The very thing written to help you overcome your despondency leaves you more despondent than ever, because it sets forth a seemingly impossible standard to reach.

This book does not intend to strip Christians of their God-given emotions, reducing them to robotic clones who grin all the time and spit out memorized scripture verses twenty-four hours a day. Rather, it intends to help the average, "normal" Christian who at times finds himself overcome and controlled by those feelings and loses his grip on the Lord in the midst of a crisis. Emotions are fine until they start robbing us of our inheritance as children of the King—and part of that inheritance is the joy of the Lord.

Speaking of emotions, when was the last time you were angry? I mean really hot? Maybe it was with your spouse or a co-worker. Perhaps it was with your boss, child, parent, or best friend. Remember how you felt? If you're like me, I remember times when (don't laugh) I actually *enjoyed* being mad! (You're smiling.) There's something almost addictive about being justifiably livid. You don't want to smile, you don't want to "kiss and make up," and you don't even want the person to apologize and ruin the good "mad" you've worked up. At that moment, the frown on your face feels good, and you would just as soon keep it there for a while. Reminds me of a sign I saw in an office where I work. I couldn't help but smile as I read it.

> *As soon as the rush is over*
> *I'm going to have a nervous breakdown.*
> *I worked for it,*
> *I owe it to myself,*
> *and no one is going to deprive me of it!*

That's how it is when we get really angry. We're mad, and we're going to enjoy it! "Don't try to make me feel better—just let me be! I deserve this one!"

Well, if we're very honest, we've all had moments

when we felt exactly the same way toward—God *(Gasp! No!)*. Yes. And usually it happens when we're stuck in another of those terrific strait places, waiting for the Lord to come to our rescue. Maybe it's a persistent problem that we feel the Lord should have taken care of long ago, and it's still around to nag and frustrate us. Or maybe it's something we have prayed and prayed and **prayed** about, yet it continues to dog our steps. Whatever, we're upset, and we don't want to hear about prayer, waiting on the Lord, or anything else "comforting."

Want to know something even more bizarre? Some of us actually know the secret to handling our aggravations and refuse to put it into action. What is this secret? Praising the Lord. I know. I've done it!

During my most recent pit stop in a strait place, my wife called me at work and attempted to ease my frustration by giving me one of those good ole' Christian pep talks that we all get when we're down and blowing it. I was hurting, and the last thing I wanted to hear was, "Try not to think negatively. Just start praising God for all His blessings, and you'll feel better." YUK! Here I am, steaming mad and bewildered at God's seeming absence in my trial, and my wife—who knows the situation better than anybody else—is telling me to, of all things, praise Him. I thought about it, and you know what? I purposely forced—that's right, *forced*—myself *not* to praise Him. Why? *Because I knew praising the Lord* WOULD *make me feel better!*

We Christians are a strange breed, aren't we? I knew praising the Lord for this blessing or that display of mercy—on top of past deliverances—would put my current problem into proper perspective, and peace would settle upon my troubled soul. I knew it because I had experienced it before! But this time I was miserable—and happy about it! I *deserved* to be miserable (I shudder to consider the truth of that statement!), and no one was going to deprive me of my misery!

What a jerk! What was I trying to prove—and to whom? If you've ever wondered why so many of us aren't getting more out of this thing called Christianity, maybe it's because we stand in our own way. We turn out to be our own greatest stumblingblock to the abundant life Christ wants us to have.

God's Word says that He inhabits the praises of Israel. See Psalm 22:3. God abides and dwells where His name is praised, and if you're feeling lately that He has packed up and gone fishing, I suggest you take a praise break. But you had better be ready for a visit. You *will* feel His presence. And as you take your eyes off the problem, it won't go away, but it will seem a lot smaller in comparison to the "big" God you love and serve.

Don't waste precious time and energy being angry at God. You know what I found out? After you've yelled, thrown things, slammed doors, and ripped foam out of the sofa, three things are still the same—you, God, and the problem. (Your apartment, however, may never be the same!) If you're angry, don't try to "fool" the Lord. He knows how you feel, whether you go around tight-lipped all day or not. Tell Him how you feel, honestly and *specifically*. Psalm 62:8 admonishes us to "pour out your heart before him." Write it down on paper if you need to, and please get down to business. Don't spend a lot of time worrying about sentence structure and proper phrasing. Talk to God as to a friend. He's your Father—not your English prof.

Then, after you've gotten everything off your chest, take it one step further—the step many of us never take. Give Him the problem and *leave* it there! Ask Jesus to take this situation and deal with it, because you can't. And ask Him for the strength not to take it back. You may have to do this more than once, but persevere. God will give you the power.

Next, *thank Him in advance for victory* in that area, and start praising Him for His goodness and just for being God. What power there is in praise! Oh that we would grab hold of this mighty spiritual weapon in the warfare with Satan!

I'm not suggesting that you'll never experience anger again. No, I just want us all to learn how to convert nonproductive reactions into positive, uplifting ones. We all need practice falling into the hands of God—learning what it means to throw our entire *weight* on the Lord. Let's begin experimenting with the Word of God. I believe Jesus is just waiting for us to try Him so He can unleash for us His mighty power for overcoming.

I challenge you to close this book after reading this chapter and purposely pray a prayer of praise to the Lord. Don't ask for anything for anybody or even for yourself. It may be tough at first, especially if the only prayers you're accustomed to praying are "gimme" prayers. You know, "Lord, gimme this and gimme that." Just begin thanking Him for all He means to you. Try it. Do it often. Not just when you're in a strait place but even when things are going great. Why not? He deserves it, doesn't He?

The McDonald's commercial is half right. You do deserve a break today—make it a praise break. I'll guarantee you will get something far better than a Big Mac.

"Shhh—"

The heaving waves slammed mercilessly against the wooden ship, sending columns of spray high into the air and over the craft's frightened occupants. Terror-filled eyes watched as the forces of nature unleashed satanic fury against the helpless craft.

"Bail! Bail!" someone shrieked above the terrific roar of the wind. The whole sea seemed alive and eager to consume the ship where the King of glory lay soundly asleep. In frantic desperation, the followers of Messiah bailed and struggled against the elements until every ounce of strength was expended. The ship was rapidly filling with water, and they were sinking. Exhausted, they surrendered to the demonic forces that threatened to destroy them, and death at sea appeared to be only moments away. The last glimmers of hope were fading fast.

Suddenly they remembered who was with them in the boat. Jesus! How could they have forgotten Him! For an instant they couldn't find Him, for "he was in the hinder part of the ship, asleep on a pillow." Mark 4:38. Imagine that! In the midst of all that chaos, confusion, and impending calamity, Jesus was taking a nap!

Quickly the disciples awakened the Lord, and with

tears in their voices they cried out, "Master, carest thou not that we perish?" Verse 38. I imagine Jesus surveyed the situation and looked out on the storm with the same expression that comes over my face when my mischievous baby daughter gets into something she has no business with—that look of parental disapproval when baby's being "naughty." He stood serenely in the face of that frenzied tempest, and with an authority only a king could possess, He lifted His hands and said simply, "Hush." The original language gives fresh insight into the phrase "peace, be still." It conjures up the image of something or someone being muzzled and rendered unable to speak. It was as if Jesus lifted His finger to His lips and, as a mother would do to a crying child, said, "Shhh—it's time to be quiet now."

The waves that only seconds earlier had all but swallowed the beleaguered craft immediately settled down and returned to a state of docile calm. The howling winds and rains that threatened to tear the vessel apart were reduced to a mere whimper and once again blew gently across Galilee. What a change took place when, at the command of Jesus, the elements rested.

The Lord of glory turned to His exhausted followers, who were staring disbelievingly at the now tranquil sea, and with disappointment in His eyes asked, "Why are ye so fearful? how is it that ye have no faith?" Verse 40. Jesus could sleep in the midst of the tempest because He knew who He was, and He knew who His Father was. The reason the disciples weren't equally at ease is that they were too busy contending with the problem to recognize that the Problem Solver was right there with them.

Over the course of the past five chapters, we have

taken an honest and sometimes lighthearted look at what makes waiting on the Lord so difficult for us. And we have considered some positive steps we may take to transform waiting to **"weighting"** on our heavenly Father. Now we add yet another rung on the ladder to practical faith and blissful rest in Jesus—the rung of being quiet.

The disciples' frantic attempts at "bailing" were an exercise in futility. All of their collective skill and expertise in sailing, acquired over years of fishing, was painfully inadequate in dealing with that typhoon. Yet in spite of the obvious, they strove and contended against the storm in their own strength until they had no more strength—and we are no different. Many Christians today seem to suffer from as many stress-related illnesses as non-Christians do. (When stressed out, I itch!) The reason? Perhaps we have yet to come to grips with who we are in Jesus and who our Father is. Perhaps we haven't learned to "hush"—to allow the Master to muzzle our fears and rest quietly in the arms of a loving God.

When we seem to be on the very brink of disaster, we would do well to heed the counsel of Psalm 37:7:

Rest in the Lord [or be silent], and wait patiently for him.

Stop "bailing," Jesus says. "Don't continue flailing and contending against the problem until your health, peace of mind, and strength are gone. Rest in Me. Be silent. Shhh." The Lord wants our attention, and He can't get it when all our energies are absorbed in wrestling against what often turns out to be the very thing He is using to bring us to Himself. He wants us to "Be still, and know" that He is God.

Psalm 46:10. When we do, amazing things begin to happen.

First, our strength is renewed. Isaiah 40:31 tells us that "they that wait upon the Lord shall renew their strength." In Hebrew, the word *wait* means to "entwine your heart around," but if that doesn't mean much to you, maybe this will. Instead of allowing your problems to tie you up in knots, tie yourself in a knot around the Lord! **Release your stranglehold on the trial, and put your strongest hold on Christ.** "Entwine your heart around" your heavenly Father, and your strength will return to you.

How do you do this? By giving Him the burden and asking Him to keep you from snatching it back with words like these: "Lord, I've fought and struggled with this thing until I'm sick of dealing with it, and I'm just plain tired. I thought I could handle it, but I can't. And even though I know I should have come to You sooner, would You please take this area of my life and deal with it in the best way for all concerned? Forgive me for taking so long and for trying to handle things my way. I see now that all I've done is make myself tired, nervous, and frustrated. I'm sorry I didn't trust You before, but now I'm placing myself and my problem in Your hands. Help me not to get anxious and take the problem from You. I want Your peace concerning this situation right now, and I thank You for it and for answering my prayer already. Amen."

This type of prayer—a prayer of surrender—"entwines" us around God. We cast ourselves into His arms, determined to hold on tight, and our strength is renewed or—as the Hebrew says—"changed" or "altered." The beauty of this scripture is clearly seen when it is understood from the original language. A possible reading could go like this: "But they that entwine their hearts around the Lord shall change their strength." Do you see it now? When we're "bailing" frantically in our own strength against the storms of life, we are assured of nothing but fatigue, frustration, and failure. But when we stop "bailing" and "latch on" to God, a supernatural transformation or "change" takes place. Suddenly, we're not facing the problem in our own puny strength anymore. We're given a "transfusion," if you please, of the power of Christ—and it is HIS divine strength that refreshes and enables us to soar like eagles over the very things that only moments before threatened to drag us in the dust! Praise God! Paul knew what he was talking about when he said:

> *Most gladly therefore will I rather glory in my infirmities, that the power of Christ may rest upon me. Therefore I take pleasure in infirmities, in reproaches, in necessities, in persecutions, in distresses for Christ's sake: for when I am weak, then am I strong.* 2 Corinthians 12:9, 10.

Another way we can "entwine our hearts around" God is to consider Jesus. The writer to the Hebrews admonishes us to "consider [reflect, look at carefully, examine, ponder] the Apostle and High Priest of our profession, Christ Jesus." Hebrews 3:1.

Take a few minutes to get your mind out of the muck and place it on the Master. Shut out all thoughts except those that relate to Jesus Christ. Reflect upon His incredible sacrifice for you. Look carefully at His life and teachings. Ponder His goodness to you, and reflect upon specific blessings you have received from Him. Think of all the things He has forgiven you for. Think of the protection He provides every day. Consider Jesus. What will happen when we do this?

[God will] keep him in perfect peace, whose mind is stayed on [Him]. Isaiah 26:3.

Now I admit right here that I have to be the world's worst meditator. My mind races a mile a minute, and it seems impossible for me to "shut up" my head long enough for me to consider Jesus. For me, I've found that "considering Jesus" at night, on my bed, with eyes closed, after a long day's work, does provide me with at least one thing—*a good night's rest!* Without fail, when I attempt this kind of meditation, I go right to sleep!

But who says meditation can take place only in the dark at the end of a long day? (This goes for prayer as well!) My times of deepest reflection usually occur in broad daylight, right at my desk, when I take a moment to look out the window and commune silently with my "Dad." Or as I walk the short distance between home and work every day.

Again, don't get hung up on methodology. One way of meditating is not more spiritual than another. It really doesn't matter *how* you consider Jesus—whether you take a walk, lie on your bed in the dark, read the Bible, listen to Christian music, or ride a pogo stick. Just take time to "be still and know," and "you will experience God's peace, which is far more wonderful than the human mind can understand. His peace will keep your thoughts and your hearts quiet and at rest as you trust in Christ Jesus." Philippians 4:7, LB.

Finally, being still enables us to hear God speaking to us. Ever notice how, when we're having a rough time of things, we have a lot to say to God about it? If we haven't talked to Him in weeks, we talk a blue streak then. But what does God have to say? What is His opinion of our predicament? Does He have any counsel or comfort to offer us?

I can just see the disciples now, yelling, "Master, we're going to drown—don't You care?" all the while bailing to beat the band. Did Jesus have anything to say? Sure He did. "Shhh"—and the storm went away. Jesus has things to say to us too when we are troubled, but we'll never hear them if we don't hush and listen.

We must individually hear Him speaking to the heart. When every other voice is hushed, and in quietness we wait before Him, the silence of the soul makes more distinct the voice of God. He bids us, "be still and know that I am God." Ps. 46:10. Here alone can true rest be found.—Ellen G. White, *The Desire of Ages*, p. 363.

Now, if you're like me, it's not often that you hear an audible voice whispering in your ear, telling you the secret things of God. I'm not saying it *never* happens. (I have a good friend who would surely jump on me if I didn't clarify what I mean.) I'm just saying that perhaps for most of us, this is an experience we don't share in too often. However, God *does* speak to each of us in our spirits and through various other ways. The Word of God comes in loud and clear, and when it does, you just "know" that it's God talking. Something inside clicks and makes you say, "Wow, that's it!" The medium will vary from person to person, as we are all unique.

I experience God speaking to me most often when I'm reading. Certain things just seem to leap off the page at me, and as the truth of a statement reaches its mark in my heart and hits home, I say silently, "Thank You, Lord. I hear You."

However, there are times when I miss the forest for the trees. I'm trying so hard to hear God speaking that I almost miss His message completely. Recently I felt a need to spend some time with my Lord talking over some things in my life that I really wanted His help with. For years I had felt a desire to work for the Lord in some full-time capacity, and while I felt the calling, I never knew to what exactly I was being called. I wanted the Lord to reveal His plan for my life to me as well as to help me resolve some financial problems my wife and I were experiencing at the time (the problem I mentioned in chapter 3).

I decided to do some fasting and praying. Four days into my fast, I was beginning to feel somewhat discouraged. The week was half over and I hadn't "heard" anything from God yet. Nothing profound had been revealed to me. No burning-bush experiences. No visitors in white. No dreams. No nothing. (I really wasn't expecting anything like that anyway.) I wasn't angry, but I was beginning to feel somewhat disappointed. Maybe the Lord had nothing to say to me on the subject. I didn't know.

On this particular day, I had taken a break at work and took along a book I had been reading—*Prophets and Kings* by Ellen G. White. Before I opened the book to where I had last stopped reading, I prayed (a habit I've developed since really coming to know Christ), asking the Lord to help me not just to read words but to change me through what I read and to let me hear Him speaking to me. The chapter

I had been reading related how the prophet Isaiah was used of God to bring messages of comfort and promises of spiritual healing if Israel should turn from idolatry and return to Jehovah. I hadn't been reading long when I came across some of the promises God was making to His people.

> *Fear thou not, for I am with thee: be not dismayed; for I am thy God: I will strengthen thee; yea, I will help thee; yea, I will uphold thee with the right hand of my righteousness. . . . I the Lord thy God will hold thy right hand, saying unto thee, Fear not; I will help thee.* Isaiah 41:10-13.

"Uh, huh. Yeah. Right," I mumbled to myself. They were familiar passages of Isaiah that I had read hundreds of times before, and, with my mind beginning to wander, I let my eyes quickly scan down the page, anxious to get on with the story and still waiting for the Lord to speak to me as I read. (I was still "bailing!")

Suddenly, a thought came zinging into my head. "Hey, slow down. Don't just skip over this stuff! Go back, and pay attention this time." (Guess where that thought came from?) I obeyed and reread the page slowly, looking for what the Lord wanted to tell me. WHAAMMO! It was as if somebody had turned the lights on! Staring me right in the face were the words, **"I AM WITH THEE: BE NOT DISMAYED. . . . I WILL HELP THEE."** "That's it! Thank You, Lord!" I exclaimed.

The message was not profound or even new, but at the right time it gave me peace concerning some uncertainties I was wrestling with. God was speaking to me, giving me assurance that all my needs, concerns for the future, and questions were being taken care of. And while specifics were not shared with me, it was enough just to know He had heard my prayers and was taking the time to reassure me of His care and presence with me. He was saying, "Shhh. Don't fret so. I'm with you, Son." What a thrill it is to hear God speak to us—to have the storm raging within calmed and muzzled under the power of His love.

How is it with you today? Have you, like the disciples, forgotten that Jesus is there with you in the midst of the storm? Have you wrestled with the trials buffeting you until you're exhausted, unsure what to do next or where to turn, and ready to throw up your hands in despair and "go down with the ship?" Wait. Don't give up yet. Put down your bucket and "hush." Be still. Jesus IS WITH YOU and IN YOU, and all the fiendish power of hell cannot swallow Him who said:

All power is given unto me in heaven and in earth. Matthew 28:18.

I am he that liveth, and was dead; and, behold, I am alive for evermore . . . and have the keys of hell and of death. Revelation 1:18.

That power is available to you today, and you can experience it right now if you will be still long enough to "entwine [yourself] about the Lord," casting your full w-e-i-g-h-t on Him. He's been there all the time, waiting for you to stop "helping" and to start "resting." Do it now. You have nothing to lose but a little frustration, a little anxiety, and a little bucket with a big hole in it.

In Paths of Righteousness

I hope by now we're all gaining a fresh perspective on what "waiting" on the Lord is all about. The nifty phrase, "attitude determines altitude" is really quite true. How I choose to respond mentally, emotionally, physically, and spiritually to life's little detours largely determines how successful I will be in dealing with the "interruption."

It is often said that "man's extremity is God's opportunity," and I would like to add, "Life's 'interruptions' often turn out to be Heaven's greatest 'productions'"—productions of His grace in our lives. Productions of His character in ours. Productions of Jesus Christ, His own dear Son, in us. God is not committed to our definition of happiness. He is, however, committed to conforming us to the image of Christ. Remember that, the next time one of God's "productions" gets under way in your life. As Paul said:

> *Though our outward man perish, yet the inward man is renewed day by day. For our light affliction, which is but for a moment, worketh for us a far more exceeding and eternal weight of glory.*
> 2 Corinthians 4:16, 17.

For it is God which worketh in you both to will and to do of his good pleasure. Philippians 2:13.

The goodness and mercy of the Lord Jesus needs to really sink into our minds and spirits. In spite of how we feel sometimes, He really isn't playing games with us. He loves us far too much for that. There is no reason to think that Jesus would go through all the agony of dying for us on the cross, only to now try to make following Him as difficult as possible by setting up an incredible series of stumblingblocks to trip us up. On the contrary, Jesus is softly and tenderly leading us in "paths of righteousness" all the way home. The question to ask yourself is not, "Is God really leading me?" but rather, "Am I following where He leads?"

A couple of years ago, I stumbled across a wonderful book written by Philip Keller—*A Shepherd Looks at Psalm 23* (Zondervan Publishing House, 1970). Keller, a former shepherd himself, takes a look at the familiar twenty-third, or shepherd's, psalm and gives insights into that chapter of scripture unlike anyone else I've ever read. Knowing the habits of sheep from first-hand experience, he parallels his experiences as a shepherd with the symbolism of the twenty-third psalm and the Christian life. The result is a fascinating and profound awakening to (1) the absolute dependence of the sheep on the shepherd and (2) the marvelous patience, love, and devotion of Christ—the Good Shepherd—toward us, the sheep.

In his chapter on Christ's leading in our lives, Keller makes this observation regarding sheep behavior:

> *Sheep are notorious creatures of habit. If left to themselves they will follow the same trails until they become ruts; graze the same hills until they turn to desert wastes; pollute their own ground until it is corrupt with disease and parasites. . . . The sheep gnaw the grass to the very ground until even the roots are damaged.*
>
> *Because of the behavior of sheep and their preference for certain favored spots, these well-worn areas become quickly infested with parasites of all kinds. In a short time a whole flock can thus become infected with worms, nematodes, and scab. The final upshot is that both land and owner are ruined while the sheep become thin, wasted, and sickly.*
>
> *The intelligent shepherd is aware of all this. . . . The greatest single safeguard which a shepherd has in handling his flock is to keep them on the move. That is to say, they dare not be left on the same ground too long.*—Pages 70-72.

Jesus knows our tendency to do our "own thing" and cling tenaciously to what *we* think is best. Like sheep, when things are going "our way" and all is well (so we think), we would be happy to remain in that place, undisturbed, forever. We get comfortable and resist tooth and nail any variance in the game plan. The Good Shepherd knows, however, that if we are left to our own devices, we will cease to grow. Our Christian development will be stunted, and our spiritual muscles will atrophy. He must keep us "on the move," leading us to new fields of experience, new plateaus of faith, and new pastures of trust and dependence.

As we wait on the Lord, we can take joy in knowing that regardless of whether we understand why we are where we are, if the Lord is our Shepherd, He is leading us over the best possible path, and we need not fret or fear.

[Jesus] has been all over this ground again and again. He knows its every advantage and every drawback. He knows where His flock will thrive and He is aware of where the feed is poor. So He acts accordingly.—Keller, pages 73, 74.

Oh, what a loving Saviour is ours! Each morning we should awaken thrilled with the eager anticipation of being led onto "higher ground" and to greener pastures with God. Our exclamation should be, "Shew me thy ways, O Lord; teach me thy paths. Lead me in thy truth, and teach me: for thou art the God of my salvation; on thee do I *wait* all the day." (Psalm 25:4, 5 emphasis supplied).

"But," I hear you saying (funny how there's always a *but*), "what if I do all the things you're suggesting and *still* nothing changes?" Suppose you start praying prayers based on God's Word and start claiming His promises? Suppose you do stop confessing the problem and start taking praise breaks. Suppose you stop "bailing" and start surrendering to God's leading in your life—and the problem is *still there*? What then?

First of all, realize that God knows

WHAT...
He's doing. He's the Good Shepherd, remember? And if He would give His life for the sheep (see John 10:11), we can rest assured that our well-being, in

every respect, is His primary concern. He is our Father, and if our earthly parents "being evil, know how to give good gifts unto [their] children, how much more shall your Father which is in heaven give good things to them that ask him." Matthew 7:11.

The Father not only knows *what* He's doing, but He knows

WHERE...

we're at and where He's going. During times of stress and testing, the temptation to ask, "Hey, God, do You know where we're going? Because I sure don't!" is overwhelming. But I'll remind you of the children of Israel crossing the Jordan River. It wasn't until their feet actually touched the water that the river parted and permitted them to continue on their way to the Promised Land. See Joshua 3, 4. To the eyes of the Israelites, the way was blocked, and I'm sure it appeared as if God had somehow become confused and didn't know where He was going. But the command to "go forward" was obeyed despite the forbidding circumstances, and the way was opened. You may be wondering what will happen next, and you may have to put your feet in the water. But don't worry—God's compass hasn't malfunctioned. He knows the way and gives you His promise:

When thou passest through the waters, I will be with thee; and through the rivers, they shall not overflow thee. Isaiah 43:2.

Our Saviour also knows

WHEN...

to move us onto new ground. God's timing is inscrutable, but always perfect. Like the disciples who struggled against the raging sea till all their strength was gone, when we feel we're at our wits' end and there's absolutely no hope left, He's there to say "Peace, be still" to the waves crashing in on us and to return our strength, renewed.

We may not always know exactly what the future holds, but as the gospel song says, we do know WHO holds the future, and if we will wholeheartedly commit our way (or, in Hebrew, "roll" our way) unto the Lord, while trusting, sincerely trusting His leading and Lordship over our lives, He promises to "bring it to pass." See Psalm 37:5. Victory, healing, maturity, peace of mind, eternal life *will* come to pass—no *ifs, ands,* or *buts* about it. We have it on God's Word, and His Word will support us if we "weight" on it.

And what of the WHY and the HOW of our situation? The reasons why we must wait on the Lord have already been explained in sufficient detail to assure us of God's goodness in permitting us to have such experiences. But more than this: in His love-marked hands are the perfect methods of bringing us to maturity as sons and daughters of God.

It is not necessary for us to understand God's leading in order to follow Him. His thoughts are not always our thoughts, neither are our ways necessarily His ways (See Isaiah 55:8), but He knows how to care for His sheep. And like Paul we can boldly declare:

I know whom I have believed, and am convinced that he is able to guard what I have entrusted to him [my life] for that day. 2 Timothy 1:12, NIV.

Finally, Jesus knows

WHO...

we are and what our situation is—even better than we know it ourselves. Love unfathomable has etched our names on the palms of His hands, and the sum of our entire lives—the highs and the lows, the mountains and the valleys—is ever before Him. See Isaiah 49:16. The "very hairs of your head are all numbered." Matthew 10:30. And you had better believe that He would not allow your pain to continue one microsecond longer than is absolutely necessary to fulfill His master plan for your life.

Psalm 139 is quickly becoming my favorite. If you have doubted God's love for you, you won't after reading this moving passage.

O Lord, you have examined my heart and know everything about me. You know when I sit or stand. When far away you know my every thought. You chart the path ahead of me, and tell me where to stop and rest. Every moment, you know where I am. You know what I am going to say before I even say it. You both precede and follow me, and place your hand of blessing on my head.

This is too glorious, too wonderful to believe! I can never be lost to your Spirit. I can never get away from my God! If I go up to heaven, you are there; if I go down to the place of the dead, you are there. If I ride the morning winds to the farthest oceans, even there your hand will guide me, your strength will support me. If I try to hide in the darkness, the night becomes light around me. For even darkness cannot hide from God; to you the night shines as bright as day. Darkness and light are both alike to you.

You made all the delicate, inner parts of my body, and knit them together in my mother's womb. Thank you for making me so wonderfully complex! It is amazing to think about. Your workmanship is marvelous—and how well I know it. You were there while I was being formed in utter seclusion! You saw me before I was born and scheduled each day of my life before I began to breathe. Every day was recorded in your Book!

How precious it is, Lord, to realize that you are thinking about me constantly! I can't even count how many times a day your thoughts turn towards me. And when I waken in the morning, you are still thinking of me! Verses 1-18, LB.

Christ indifferent to our cries for help? Confused as to what is best for us? Playing games with our lives and unaware of our needs, hurts, and desires? I'm ashamed to write it, ashamed to entertain the thought.

Neither our lives nor our "ways" are left to chance. With God there is no such thing as "luck" (good or bad) or "fate." "The steps of a good man are ordered by the Lord: and he delighteth in his way." Psalm 37:23. Sound like a roll of the dice? No. Our steps—the direction and course of our lives—are established by One who cannot err, and those who love and serve Him actually "delight" in following the path He has marked out.

What happens when we follow the righteous paths Christ leads us in? "Though he fall, he shall not be utterly cast down: for the Lord upholdeth him with his hand." Verse 24. Praise God! We may, because of our sheeplike tendency to go our own ways, occasionally "fall" into despondency, sin, or some other

IN PATHS OF RIGHTEOUSNESS

"strait place." But in spite of being temporarily "down," we are not "out!" The Lord Himself, our Good Shepherd, is right there beside us to hold us up with His mighty hand. How wonderfully blessed we are!

Is the Lord, Jesus Christ, your Shepherd? If He's not, why not bow your head right now and ask Him to forgive you for going your own way (see Isaiah 53:6) and to lead you now in His way—in paths of righteousness? If the Lord is your Shepherd, don't waste another second doubting His divine guidance and care for you. The way of the cross leads home, and if you remain on the path He has marked out for you, you will reach that heavenly shore. Won't you join me in this prayer:

Search me, O God, and know my heart: try me, and know my thoughts: and see if there be any wicked way in me, and lead me in the way everlasting. Psalm 139:23, 24.

In all thy ways [your hopes, your trials, your plans, your ambitions, your joys, your sorrows, your business dealings, your leisure, your finances, your family planning, your courtships, your marriage—in ALL your ways] acknowledge him, and he shall direct thy paths. Proverbs 3.6.

Lead on, Gentle Shepherd. Lead on!

On Eagle's Wings

High Flight

Oh! I have slipped the surly bonds of earth
  And danced the skies on laughter-silvered wings;
Sunward I've climbed, and joined the tumbling mirth
  Of sun-split clouds—and done a hundred things
You have not dreamed of—wheeled and soared and swung
  High in the sunlit silence. Hov'ring there,
I've chased the shouting wind along, and flung
  My eager craft through footless halls of air.
Up, up the long delirious, burning blue
  I've topped the wind-swept heights with easy grace
Where never lark, or even eagle flew—
  And, while with silent lifting mind I've trod
The high, untrespassed sanctity to space,
  Put out my hand and touched the face of God.

> —Pilot Officer John Gillespie Magee, Jr.
> R.C.A.F.

For several years now I have enjoyed the filmed rendition of this moving poem on television. One of the local networks uses "High Flight" early each morning, prior to the playing of the national anthem, to signal the end of another day of broadcasting. It's the same each time. First, the station's logo appears on the screen. There's soft music playing in the background, and the announcer's voice is heard thanking the viewers for watching. After giving instruction on where to turn on the radio for further broadcasting from that network, he bids all a Good night. The next thing you see is a runway with a jet fighter plane hurtling down its length. The scream of the powerful engines surging to take-off speed is soon matched with some inspirational background music, evoking a stirring feeling of thrill and expectancy. The craft takes to the air, and for the next sixty seconds or so, you believe you are right there next to pilot officer Magee in the cockpit of that majestic silver bird, experiencing the incredible splendor and freedom of flight! I love it!

I sit there totally captivated by the sight of this supersonic war plane—an otherwise grim symbol of destruction—transformed into a seemingly live object of grace and majestic strength, waltzing through space in a fantastic aerial ballet. No secret missions, no hypersonic raids, no strategic maneuvers. Just flying for the unadulterated pleasure and sheer delight of flying—of soaring—of being *free!*

This feeling, this mental image of mounting the skies on the wings of an eagle, is what I want to leave you with as we come to the close of this book.

One of the saddest sights you'll ever see is a bird, either caged or because of some injury, no longer able to fly. The sight is sad because you realize that this creature, meant to scale the heavens, can no longer enjoy that freedom and must spend the remainder of its days bound to the earth—grounded.

But perhaps even sadder is the sight of so many "caged," "grounded" Christians. They can be observed in prolific numbers in churches all over the world. They're quite easy to spot, and high-powered binoculars aren't required to obtain a good close-up of this peculiar bird. In fact, for some of you, you'll get your closest look in your bathroom mirror! This is not a put-down. Rather, it is a sad commentary on the fact that so many of God's children—His blood-bought pearls of great price, heirs to all that heaven can offer—know precious little of the abundant life in Jesus and what it means to "mount up with wings like an eagle." Maybe your church is an exception. I pray to God it is. But chances are good that if you look around at the faces of your fellow worshipers next Sabbath, you'll see expressions similar to those you might see on a caged eagle. Though eagles may not have expressive faces like humans, you can see a sadness in their eyes—a painful acceptance of the knowledge that they will never again know the freedom of flight and that, consequently, they are destined to a life of doleful earth dwelling. The look in the eyes of many Christians is slightly different, however. It is a look, not of lamentation over never being able to fly *again,* but of *never having known what it is to fly!*

God's Word tells us that those who "entwine their hearts around [weight on] Him" will soar like eagles, run and not be weary, walk and not faint. How many "tired" Christians roost on our church pews from week to week? How many are weary of well-doing, "trying to make it," and are fainting under the yoke of an insipid, tasteless religion that makes little or no impact on their everyday lives, supplying only dead formalism, redundant ritual, and meaningless routine? Why is it this way for so many? I believe it is because we've allowed "religion" to take the place of Christianity. The two are different, you know.

In his book *Living God's Joy* (Pacific Press Publishing Association, 1979), Douglas Cooper makes this distinction:

> *Religion is men struggling, reaching out, to try to find something bigger than themselves—a god or even God, if you please. Religion is men searching for something. Christianity is God searching for men.*
>
> *Christians say that men have not found God, but rather that God has found them. How fascinating that for men to meet and experience God, they were not expected first to struggle to become like Him. Instead, so that they would have a way to enter again into His presence, He became like them!...*
>
> *Christianity is a burden all right—the kind of burden sails are to a ship or wings are to a bird!*—Pages 24, 25.

The reason our experience with Christ is a ho-hum, dry, lifeless ordeal to be endured once a week for an excruciating hour and a half is that we're not experiencing *Christ* at all! We're experiencing "religion" instead—and the more we "try to be good" and "try" to be like Jesus, the more we clip our spiritual wings and come crashing to the earth with a thud instead of soaring like eagles. Formalism, ritual, and "going through the motions" can never substitute for a daily, hourly encounter with the living Christ. And if you're ever to transcend the status quo brand of religion which robs so many of the joy of the Lord, start refusing to settle for anything less than all you're entitled to as a child of God.

Take the attitude of Beethoven, the famous composer, who lost his hearing but not his thirst for life. While sitting at his piano one day, he was overheard shouting at the top of his lungs, "I will take life by the throat!" Or better still, take Jacob's attitude as he wrestled with Jesus all night. "And he said, I will not let thee go, except thou bless me." Genesis 32:26. Don't settle for second-hand faith—for second best. Determine to seize life by the throat, draining every precious drop of it. "Weight" on the Lord. Fling your all into His hands and refuse to let go until you receive the blessing you stand in need of. Begin pursuing a relationship with Christ that is more than duty and more than obligation. Discover the freedom— yes, **freedom,** of serving and following God for the sheer delight and unadulterated joy of loving and being with Him!

You are a child of God! You were never meant to go through this life just getting by. You were born (again) to fly!

I am come that they might have life, and that they might have it more abundantly. John 10:10.

Don't just read words. Did you catch that word *abundantly?* It means, "beyond," "excessive," "beyond measure," "overflowing," "superabundant in quantity and superior in quality!" Jesus wants to break the shackles that keep us "grounded" and set us free to a life that soars above the crowd. A life

ON EAGLE'S WINGS 61

overflowing with joy. A life with peace "beyond measure." A life "exceedingly" filled with love "beyond" the human imagination—"superabundant in quantity and superior in quality!"

Church of Christ, how can we be content with only a "form of godliness"? *Abundance* is the inheritance of the Christian. Salvation from sin is not all there is! Don't stop there. Keep going. The best is yet to come—and you don't have to wait until you enter the turnstiles at the pearly gates to get your wings. "Beloved, ***NOW*** are we the sons of God!" 1 John 3:2. "The Lord is [our] portion . . . ; therefore will [we] hope in him." Lamentations 3:24. We cannot be content with existence as paupers when the Lord Himself is our inheritance. Those born again into the family of God are the richest people on earth, and no trial, no circumstance, no perplexity can sever our union with the Father. See Romans 8:35-39.

But what happens when I don't soar with eagle's wings? What am I supposed to do when I'm so weighed down with burdens I can hardly lift my head, let alone my spirit? Let us take a lesson from the eagle herself.

Regular daily movement, whether within the eagle's territory or on migration, is usually achieved with a minimum of effort, little wing flapping, and by using thermals [a rising column of air, caused by the uneven heating of the earth or sea by the sun] and mountain updraughts. In any windy mountainous area, powerful standing waves of air swiftly lift an eagle to any desired height with little effort.

Having risen on a thermal to several thousand feet above flat country the eagle then sets its

> *wings to a gentle downward glide and shoots off in the desired direction. Its glide may carry it many miles without interruption; or it may use another good thermal to regain height before its first momentum is fully spent. In either case it rarely flaps its wings, but conserves energy by using currents to rise by soaring or circling, and then gliding without effort.*—Leslie Brown, *Eagles of the World* (Universe Books, 1976), pp. 81-83.

The very thing that is potentially resistant to flight (the winds), the eagle is able to use to gain height and soar. So it can be with us. We need not view the trials that come into our lives as enemies—unwelcomed winds whipping us into helpless submission. As we learn to shift our "weight" on the Lord, surrendering to His currents of love, those same winds we thought would surely destroy us can be transformed into thermals of faith that will lift us to the very throne of God. When you're assailed by Satan's gusts of discouragement, don't "flap your wings" and struggle in your own strength. Shift your gaze heavenward, stretch forth on the wings of prayer and praise, and glide all the way to Jesus.

One day soon Jesus is coming back to take home with Him a very special people. These people will know what it means to "weight" on the Lord.

> *In the spiritual world those who will stand for God at the climax of earth's history will be a group extraordinarily like Jesus Christ. They will be experts at loving. They will be full of unquenchable joy. They will live lives of continual victory.*

> *Amid the darkening shadows of earth's last night, they will reflect the saving light of God's love more splendidly than has any group of God's people since Creation.*
>
> *The spiritual development God's people will finally achieve will be gained not artificially by their own struggles to be good [dead religion], but naturally by the closeness of their walk with God. They concentrate on this closeness to achieve success.*—Douglas Cooper, *Living in Our Finest Hour* (Pacific Press Publishing Association, 1982), pp. 24, 25.

These special ones have learned to be patient in trial. They have learned how to "fall into the hands of God," thereby transforming strait places into steppingstones to the high places. Their lips are accustomed to praising His name in the valley as well as on the mountaintop. They have listened for and heard the voice of God speaking to their hearts in the silence of their souls. They have refused to allow the Bible to be just a book of famous quotes from famous people. They have rejected a "name only" brand of Christianity and have "seized" the promises of God, their inheritance as sons, and the abundant life by the throat, believing all that heaven has to offer is for them. They have "tasted" for themselves and seen that He is good. They have established an extraordinary closeness with the King of kings. And because of all this, when Christ does part the sky, descending in clouds of glory with the trump of God echoing throughout the expanse of the entire universe, it will only be natural for those saints living and dead to obediently and lovingly respond to that voice of triumphant invitation beckoning them to "come away" and be His bride.

They ran a good race and did not become weary. They walked in paths of righteousness and did not faint. And now, after having soared with Him in this life, it is not at all difficult for them to stretch forth their wings once more in response to the One whom they have learned to trust and to "mount up" to the loving side of their friend, Jesus.

Is it your desire not only to be "caught up together with them in the clouds" (see 1 Thessalonians 4:17) on that final and great day, but to be "caught up" with Him now? Are you ready to cast off the shackles of doubt, anxiety, dead works, and second-hand faith that "grounds" you to this dark world, and start casting yourself, your trials, your "everything" into the hands of God? There's no better place, you know. In His hand, nothing can touch you except Him. Bring your burdens and your failures. Lay them down and rest—in His hand!

Do it now. Don't delay. He promises that you will not be disappointed. My prayer is that you will—

Grow in grace, and in the knowledge of our Lord and Saviour Jesus Christ. 2 Peter 3:18.

—And that you will allow that knowledge to make you—

Steadfast, unmovable, always abounding in the work of the Lord. 1 Corinthians 15:58.

As you grow and as you abound, remember always to *"Wait on the Lord: be of good courage, and he shall strengthen thine heart: [WEIGHT], I say, on the Lord!"* Psalm 27:14.